# EXPLORING
# the Sunday
# Gospel

## A Lectionary-Based
## Guide for Groups
## (Cycle A)

Rev. Joseph T. Sullivan

LIGUORI
PUBLICATIONS

ONE LIGUORI DRIVE
LIGUORI, MO 63057-9999
(314) 464-2500

Imprimi Potest:
James Shea, C.SS.R.
Provincial, St. Louis Province
The Redemptorists

Imprimatur:
Monsignor Maurice F. Byrne
Vice Chancellor, Archdiocese of St. Louis

ISBN 0-89243-482-1
Library of Congress Catalog Card Number: 92-75937

Cover and interior art by Christine Kraus

# Contents

# INTRODUCTION

The Spirit that refreshed the Church through the Second Vatican Council calls us to a respectful awareness of Scripture and an application of the gospel in our daily lives:

"Seeing that, in sacred Scripture, God speaks through men in human fashion, it follows that the interpreter of sacred Scriptures, if he is to ascertain what God has wished to communicate to us, should carefully search out the meaning which the sacred writers really had in mind, that meaning which God had thought well to manifest through the medium of their words."

*Dogmatic Constitution on Divine Revelation (#12)*

"Only the light of faith and meditation on the Word of God can enable us to find everywhere and always the God 'in whom we live and exist' (Acts 17:28); only thus can we seek his will in everything, see Christ in all men, acquaintance or stranger, make sound judgments on the true meaning and value of temporal realities both in themselves and in relation to man's end."

*Decree on the Apostolate of Lay People (#4)*

*Exploring the Sunday Gospel* is a structured opportunity for small groups of Christians to break open the word of God, to understand its rich depth, and to discern how the word is and can be made manifest in the world. It is an opportunity to gather as one, in the name of Jesus, and pray with that week's gospel: "For where two or three are gathered together in my name, there am I in the midst of them" (Matthew 18:20).

## BASIC GUIDELINES

Select an appropriate hour on a regular weekly basis. Consider this hour a priority. It is an occasion for God's grace. It should be unhurried and prayerful. "But as for the seed that fell on rich soil, they are the ones who, when they have heard the word, embrace it with a generous and good heart, and bear fruit through perseverance" (Luke 8:15).

Time and place for gathering can vary according to the needs of the group. Participants should bring their own Bible, their own preferred translation. A variety of translations will broaden discussion.

Because facilitating the group takes no preparation, someone should be invited (or volunteer) to facilitate each week. Be sure everyone who wishes to facilitate is given the opportunity.

Simple refreshments add to a sense of communion.

## THE FORMAT

Each week opens with a prayer: "We Gather in Prayer." You will notice that the prayer reflects the theme of the gospel for that week. You will also notice that the prayer is incomplete. Allow those in the group to expand the prayer according to individual, community, and global needs.

After the gathering prayer, the facilitator reads all or part of the gospel for that week ("Read...") and asks someone to read the reflection that follows ("Reflect"). The reflection rephrases the reading and expands on the theme.

The facilitator then leads the group in considering two questions ("Consider") that are designed to break open the word beyond what the reading and reflection offer. There are no right or wrong responses to these questions. Their purpose is to help the group mine the full richness of the word.

Next, the facilitator slowly and reverently invites the group into personal petitions ("Let Us Pray"). The list provided reflects the theme of the reading. The last petition allows each person in the group to focus on specific needs (shared with the group or held silently before the Lord). Before the petitions are shared, the group should decide on a common response: "Lord, hear our prayer," "Graciously hear us, O Lord," or any response the group feels is appropriate.

The period of reflective silence ("A Reflective Moment of Silence") offers the group a time for deep intimacy with God. This period may feel awkward at first. With time, however, it will become natural. The facilitator should judge when it's time to invite the group for refreshments (if provided) and further activities or discussions ("Additional Activities/Discussion").

The group may wish to place a picture of Jesus or a crucifix on a table in the center of the gathering. Flowers, in season, even artificial flowers, add to the atmosphere. A lighted candle enhances the environment as well. These and other details help create a mood conducive to prayer and reflection.

## GROWING IN FAITH

Maturity and growth take time. We notice the beauty of trees and shrubs and flowers, but we do not see them grow. Only after weeks and months do we perceive their cycle of life.

Christian maturing evolves in the same imperceptible manner. *Exploring the Sunday Gospel* can be instrumental in that process.

# The Season of ADVENT

# First Sunday of
# ADVENT

*...you also must be prepared...*
Matthew 24:44

## WE GATHER IN PRAYER

Lord, bless us with spirit and enthusiasm. Help us get into the spirit of the season as we look forward to celebrating the birth of your Son.

It is through Jesus that we come to you, the source of our joy and happiness. Flood our souls with your grace...

### Amen

## READ MATTHEW 24:37-44

### REFLECT

Jesus cautions his followers not to be careless and indifferent when it comes to relating to God. Jesus uses the experience of Noah to show how the "ho-hum" attitude had preceded the Flood that destroyed the earth. He challenges his listeners to realize the importance of time, to reflect on how time has played a role in the faith experience of others, and to respect the role that time plays in the journey of a faithful disciple.

In effect, Jesus says, "Live as if these are your last hours." Let no opportunity of grace escape you; let no sin seize you.

### CONSIDER

- What might have been the reaction of the crowd as they listened to Jesus' comments about the "coming of the Son of Man" (24:39)?
- Do we live today as if these were our "last hours"? Why or why not?

### LET US PRAY

- For ourselves, that we will keep Jesus as the center of our Advent season
- For those of us who are careless and indifferent about our faith journeys
- For all Christians, that we will give witness to Jesus especially during the season of Advent
- For the grace and wisdom to celebrate the sacrament of reconciliation during this Advent season
- For our own personal intentions (shared with the group or held silently before the Lord)

### A REFLECTIVE MOMENT OF SILENCE

### ADDITIONAL ACTIVITIES/DISCUSSION

- Let's share our individual ideas about the end of time.
- Why is indifference a major threat to our spiritual growth?

# Second Sunday of
# ADVENT

*"You brood of vipers!"*
Matthew 3:7

## WE GATHER IN PRAYER

Lord, when John the Baptist preached, he put bite into his remarks. He was not hesitant; he meant business.

Bless our souls with this same courage, this same conviction about who Jesus is and the role he plays in our lives. Give us the grace to respond to John's urgent directions to repent...

## Amen

## READ MATTHEW 3:1-12

## REFLECT

Jesus' cousin, John, preaches to great numbers. The crowd flocks to hear his message—a harsh message that is demanding and challenging. John is trying to convince his listeners that if they expect to be well-disposed toward the Messiah when he finally comes, they must repent of the evil they've done and are doing.

John appears to be angry with the Pharisees and Sadducees, the two principle religious groups of Jesus' day. In this account, the Pharisees and Sadducees join the crowd, but their hearts are not sincere.

## CONSIDER
- What is a viper and why does John use this label in reference to the Pharisees and Sadducees?
- John is preaching to us today. What is he saying?

## LET US PRAY
- For great blessings of mind and heart during this Advent season
- For our own families and all families in our parish
- For those of us who are weak in faith
- For the humility to repent
- For our own personal intentions (shared with the group or held silently before the Lord)

## A REFLECTIVE MOMENT OF SILENCE

## ADDITIONAL ACTIVITIES/DISCUSSION
- How can our group witness to Jesus the way John did?
- Of what do we need to repent? Of what does our society need to repent?

# Third Sunday of
# ADVENT

*"Go and tell..."*
Matthew 11:4

## WE GATHER IN PRAYER

Lord, as we look forward to celebrating Jesus' birth, help us to be mindful of everything that Jesus did for us. With his life, he offered us eternity.

Open our eyes to the wonders and miracles in our midst every day. Let us see Christ in everyone we meet...

## Amen

## READ MATTHEW 11:2-11

### REFLECT

Jesus tells John's followers to read the signs, to draw their own conclusions. He invites everyone to look around, to see the blind gaining their sight, the lame walking, the lepers becoming clean.

But Jesus doesn't stop with a mere invitation to look around at the wonders; he says, "Go and tell..." (11:4). Jesus challenges John's disciples to think about what they see, to reflect on the signs around them, and to draw conclusions of their own.

### CONSIDER

- Is there enough "evidence" for the disciples of John to conclude that Jesus is the long-awaited Messiah?
- Why would Jesus say, "And blessed is the one who takes no offense at me" (11:6)?

### LET US PRAY

- For those of us who want to take Jesus more seriously by studying his life and his teachings
- For all of us who are handicapped in our faith, that we may overcome the obstacles to a sound belief in Jesus
- For the same kind of compassion and kindness in our hearts that Jesus manifested to everyone
- For our families, that we be open to the graces of the Advent season
- For our own personal intentions (shared with the group or held silently before the Lord)

## A REFLECTIVE MOMENT OF SILENCE

## ADDITIONAL ACTIVITIES/DISCUSSION

- How are we disciples of both Jesus and John?
- What one major factor is considered both a sign and a cause of Christian unity?

# Fourth Sunday of

# ADVENT

*...he did as the angel of the Lord had commanded him...*
Matthew 1:24

## WE GATHER IN PRAYER

Lord, during this holy season, help us to see your divine plan unfolding. Help us to trust that your will for our lives is one of peace.

As we reflect on the roles Mary and Joseph played in your plan for redemption, guide our hearts to search for our own roles...

## Amen

## READ MATTHEW 1:18-24

### REFLECT

Joseph is understandably upset. Yet, believing in the will of God, he responds with tenderness to the invitation of the angel to embrace Mary as his wife and to be the father of her child.

Mary and Joseph know something that the rest of the world needs to know; they know that God is invested in our day-to-day lives. They know the meaning of "Emmanuel," God-with-us.

### CONSIDER

- Compare the message the angel gave Joseph and the message the angel gave Mary.
- How does this gospel contribute to our excitement for the birth of Christ?

### LET US PRAY

- For a sense of awe and respect that God would become one of us
- For pregnant women, that they too may have awe and respect for the new life in their womb
- For a profound respect for the name of Jesus
- For our families, that we all respect the dignity of all life forms
- For our own personal intentions (shared with the group of held silently before the Lord)

### A REFLECTIVE MOMENT OF SILENCE

### ADDITIONAL ACTIVITIES/DISCUSSION

- How do Christmas carols and Advent songs add to or detract from our appreciation for this time of year?
- What role do angels play in our faith journey today?

# The Season of
# CHRISTMAS

# CHRISTMAS DAY

## WE GATHER IN PRAYER

Lord, thank you for the wonder of this holy day. Thank you for placing the power of your Word in our midst. We behold the light of Jesus piercing the darkness and marvel at his peace.

Lead us in ways, Lord, that celebrate this day every day of our lives. Place in our hearts a Christmas spirit for every day of the year...

Amen

## READ JOHN 1:1-18

### REFLECT

John talks like a philosopher. He does not give a descriptive narrative of what happened in Bethlehem; Matthew, Mark, and Luke cover that part of history. John tells us about other aspects of this event in salvation history.

John says that no one has seen God—but they have seen Jesus. This is a revelation. God draws back the curtain and, in effect, says, "Here I am."

### CONSIDER

■ Why is this an appropriate gospel for Christmas day?

■ "The true light, which enlightens everyone, was coming into the world" (1:9). Does that include people who are not Christian? Why?

### LET US PRAY

■ For all people, that hearts and minds are touched with God's love throughout the year

■ For a stronger faith, that our joy as Christians becomes evident to the world

■ For generous hearts, that we may respond to the needs of the poor all year long

■ For the grace to be compassionate

■ For our own personal intentions (shared with the group or held silently before the Lord)

## A REFLECTIVE MOMENT OF SILENCE

## ADDITIONAL ACTIVITIES/DISCUSSION

■ What plans can we make to celebrate the Christmas season beyond Christmas day?

■ As a small Christian community celebrating the birth of Christ, let's share a special treat.

# (Sunday in the Octave of Christmas)
# HOLY FAMILY

*"...flee..."*
Matthew 2:13

## WE GATHER IN PRAYER

Lord, open our hearts to reflect on the little family in which you nestled your Son. May we see their human fear, confusion, uncertainty—and hope.

Bless us with that same kind of faith. Teach us to reverence your divine providence...

### Amen

## READ MATTHEW 2:13-15,19-23

### REFLECT

Like many families today, the Holy Family is on the run. They're not jumping from meetings to ball games to school functions—but they are certainly busy. They are refugees.

Joseph, faithful to his mission, responds to the Lord's urgent guidance to flee. He does not calculate how he and his family will survive; he does not weigh the advantages and disadvantages of "relocating." He does not consider himself immune to the struggles of life.

### CONSIDER

■ What parallels exist between this account and the life of Moses? (See Exodus 2.)

■ How does this gospel celebrate the Holy Family?

### LET US PRAY

■ For the holiness of all families

■ For great blessings on parents, that they may be strong in their faith commitments

■ For great blessings on children, that they may respond with playful hope to God's invitation to life

■ For kindness and patience

■ For our own personal intentions (shared with the group or held silently before the Lord)

## A REFLECTIVE MOMENT OF SILENCE

## ADDITIONAL ACTIVITIES/DISCUSSION

■ Do we know a person who is or has been a refugee? Can we invite this person to share his/her experiences with us?

■ Difficulties and trials may be steppingstones to holiness. What does this statement mean?

## Octave of Christmas (New Year's Day)

# MARY, MOTHER OF GOD

*...Mary kept all these things...*
Luke 2:19

### WE GATHER IN PRAYER

Lord, teach us to look beyond ourselves, to model Mary in our life of faith. Open our eyes to the mystery of you in our day-to-day lives.

Like Mary, may we reflect on our life experiences to find your wisdom and direction. Draw our attention outward, to the needs of others...

Amen

### READ LUKE 2:16-21

### REFLECT

In this brief reading, we see the shepherds arriving; Mary is curious. The shepherds tell of the angel's announcement; Mary is amazed.

Mary is an observer of life. She knows that her role as the mother of this child is somehow significant, but she has no blueprint to follow; she only has the clues of life as they unfold around her. Mary knows that her role is to "pay attention"—and she does.

### CONSIDER

■ What other details might Mary have observed that are not specifically mentioned in this reading?

■ Why is this reading selected for this particular feast?

### LET US PRAY

■ For a peaceful faith in Mary, the Mother of Jesus

■ For a profound faith in Mary, the Mother of God

■ For an appreciation of Mary's role in the salvation of all people

■ For the inspiration and courage to follow Mary's example

■ For our own personal intentions (shared with the group or held silently before the Lord)

### A REFLECTIVE MOMENT OF SILENCE

### ADDITIONAL ACTIVITIES/DISCUSSION

■ What Marian devotions are particularly meaningful to us?

■ How can we become observers of life, looking beyond ourselves? How will this affect our faith?

# Second Sunday After
# CHRISTMAS

*...full of grace and truth.*
John 1:14

## WE GATHER IN PRAYER

Lord, let us never forget that you are always with us. May our hearts be grateful for the life and light of Christ present to us today—and through all time.

We want to bear your Word to the world, but we are painfully aware of our human limitations. We rely on your constant wisdom to light our way...

### Amen

## READ JOHN 1:1-18

### REFLECT

This gospel is the same gospel that is read at Mass on Christmas day. Since the Church invites us to consider it again, it must be significant.

The theme of this gospel is the Word going forth, shining in the darkness, dwelling among us. As Christians, that is our mission as well. This gospel points us in the direction of the kingdom. We look outward, into the darkness, into the very midst of the world around us. As Christians, we are enlightened with the light and life of Christ; we get involved.

### CONSIDER

- In light of the previous comments, why is this a significant gospel?
- Verse 5 states, "The darkness has not overcome it." Do conditions in the world today indicate that the darkness just might overcome the Light?

### LET US PRAY

- For all educators, that they may be touched with God's wisdom and patience
- For open minds and open hearts
- For the courage to bear Christ's light to the world
- For the ability to discern true Christian values
- For our own personal intentions (shared with the group or held silently before the Lord)

## A REFLECTIVE MOMENT OF SILENCE

## ADDITIONAL ACTIVITIES/DISCUSSION

- Is there a special concern in our community that merits our attention as a Christian community taking the gospel seriously?
- What distinguishes a Christian value from a humanitarian value?

# EPIPHANY

*...they set out...*
Matthew 2:9

## WE GATHER IN PRAYER

Lord, when we tire along our journey to you, be our strength. Fill our hearts with the same faith and determination displayed by the magi. They sought you; they were single-hearted in their goal.

May we, too, set the eyes of our souls on you. With single-hearted purpose, may we seek you all the days of our lives...

### Amen

## READ MATTHEW 2:1-12

### REFLECT

The magi are astrologers. They have identified a celestial phenomena and are determined to honor its significance.

In this account, there are conflicting determinations. Herod is determined to destroy the child; the magi are determined to honor the child. Herod's determination, self-centered and fear-driven, leads to violence and death. The magi's determination, other-directed and driven by faith, leads to life.

### CONSIDER

■ Why, do you suppose, are the astrologers so determined to follow the star?

■ How might the astrologers' determination have affected Herod's thinking and ultimate choices?

### LET US PRAY

■ For those of us who feel tremendous insecurity, that we may find peace in our faith

■ For all of humanity, that evil motives may lose their grip on the human heart

■ For all who actively search for God

■ For an increase in the gifts of the Holy Spirit, especially wisdom

■ For our own personal intentions (shared with the group or held silently before the Lord)

## A REFLECTIVE MOMENT OF SILENCE

## ADDITIONAL ACTIVITIES/DISCUSSION

■ What gifts (time, skill, services) can we offer others in the name of Jesus?

■ What is the difference between determination and stubbornness?

# BAPTISM OF THE LORD

*"...allow it now...."*
Matthew 3:15

## WE GATHER IN PRAYER

Lord, who are we in your sight? We know; we are your beloved children. Who are we in our own sight? That is a more accurate question.

Teach us the meaning of love, O God, of what it means to be loved and called by you...

Amen

## READ MATTHEW 3:13-17

### REFLECT

The setting is the Jordan River. The crowds mill around, and the power of the Spirit fills the air. Jesus approaches John and asks to be baptized. John, recognizing Jesus, insists that Jesus should baptize him.

But Jesus knows his own personal role. He knows that something in the unfolding of God's plan for salvation calls for him to be baptized by John. At this early point in his ministry, Jesus knows himself as servant.

### CONSIDER
- Why does Jesus insists on John baptizing him?
- What is the significance of this gospel?

### LET US PRAY
- For a spirit of honesty and humility
- For a sincere desire to love God perfectly
- For the wisdom to know and the courage to admit our shortcomings
- For all those who suffer with illusions of self-importance
- For our own personal intentions (shared with the group or held silently before the Lord)

### A REFLECTIVE MOMENT OF SILENCE

### ADDITIONAL ACTIVITIES/DISCUSSION
- Let's discuss how psychology supports and/or confuses our faith journeys.
- How can we better discover who we are as children of God?

The Season of
LENT

# First Sunday in
# LENT

*The tempter approached...*
Matthew 4:3

## WE GATHER IN PRAYER

Lord, we know the confusion and fear of temptation approaching. We know the weaknesses of our human condition and place those weaknesses into your keeping.

Be our confidence when our weaknesses threaten to defeat us. Walk with us through this season of Lent...

### Amen

## READ MATTHEW 4:1-11

### REFLECT

After fasting in the desert for forty days and forty nights, Jesus is very much in touch with his human weaknesses. He knows he is at the "end of his rope," so to speak. With that awareness, he is able to recognize the empty promises of the tempter; he remains faithful to his God.

With this same kind of awareness in the face of temptation, we can remain faithful. Knowing our limits, knowing we need God's strength and wisdom, knowing we are basically helpless, helps us cooperate with grace when temptations are attractive.

### CONSIDER

■ How do the temptations of Jesus resemble the tests Israel faced? (See Deuteronomy 8:3, 6:16, and 6:13.)

■ What is the message of this gospel and how does it apply to the season of Lent?

### LET US PRAY

■ For a strong faith

■ For a meaningful Lent

■ For the humility to admit we are weak

■ For God's help in resisting temptations

■ For our own personal intentions (shared with the group or held silently before the Lord)

## A REFLECTIVE MOMENT OF SILENCE

## ADDITIONAL ACTIVITIES/DISCUSSION

■ What do we know about the experience of hunger?

■ Let's agree to a discipline of fasting for this season of Lent.

# Second Sunday in
# LENT

*...he was transfigured...*
Matthew 17:2

## WE GATHER IN PRAYER

Lord, help us remember that you are with us at all times. Teach us to draw on your strength when things are difficult as well as when things are fine.

Inspire each of us to open ourselves to your grace ever available to us. Especially during this Lenten season, may we recognize your glory and presence...

### Amen

## READ MATTHEW 17:1-9

## REFLECT

Jesus and his three friends are alone on the mountain. They are far from the crush and roar of the crowd. Jesus is then "transfigured," changed. His face shines like the sun. This gospel tells us that Jesus' clothes become dazzling white.

There are no "special effects" going on here; this is God in the midst of the human experience—and human beings recognizing that fact.

## CONSIDER
- Why are Peter, James, and John filled with fear?
- How does the Transfiguration support the apostles for their future mission?

## LET US PRAY
- For ourselves, that our faith can embrace the splendor of the Transfiguration
- For God's grace, that we will continue with our Lenten resolutions
- For a renewed appreciation of Christ present in the Eucharist
- For a loving heart, that we may see the goodness of Jesus in others
- For our own personal intentions (shared with the group or held silently before the Lord)

## A REFLECTIVE MOMENT OF SILENCE

## ADDITIONAL ACTIVITIES/DISCUSSION
- How might God "transfigure" our own lives?
- What role does prayer play in the experience of transfiguration?

# Third Sunday in
# LENT

*"Our ancestors worshiped on this mountain..."*
John 4:20

## WE GATHER IN PRAYER

God, when Jesus speaks directly to our hearts, offering himself to us, help us to believe. When he offers us "a spring of water welling up to eternal life" (4:14), may we feel our thirst being quenched.

May the living water of your wisdom, Lord, help us see your truth in the faith traditions of all people...

### Amen

## READ JOHN 4:5-42

## REFLECT

Samaria is a hostile territory; there is religious friction between the Samaritans and the Jewish people. Yet, Jesus ventures into Samaritan land and engages the people in dialogue, offering them the Good News of salvation.

Jesus explains that God is to be worshiped correctly: in spirit and in truth. He focuses on the root of the faith rather than the external trappings.

## CONSIDER

- What does Jesus mean when he says, "The reaper is already receiving his payment and gathering crops for eternal life, so that the sower and reaper can rejoice together" (4:36)?
- What significance does this gospel have to our Lenten journey?

## LET US PRAY

- For sincerity in our worship
- For an appreciation of our own Catholic traditions as well as the traditions of other faiths
- For all of us who search for God with sincere hearts
- For the courage to accept on faith what we cannot understand
- For our own personal intentions (shared with the group or held silently before the Lord)

## A REFLECTIVE MOMENT OF SILENCE

## ADDITIONAL ACTIVITIES/DISCUSSION

- What do we know about other faith traditions and how do we appreciate or fail to appreciate them?
- Let's invite someone to share their experience of "being saved."

# Fourth Sunday in
# LENT

*"I was blind and now I see."*
John 9:25

## WE GATHER IN PRAYER

Lord, in your gentle way, unveil to us that which blinds us, that which keeps us from seeing things as they are. Bless us with objectivity and justice.

Draw us to yourself, Lord, as we open ourselves to respect others, to listen to their truths...

## Amen

## READ JOHN 9:1-41

### REFLECT

This gospel is melodramatic. If it were embellished, it would make a great novel. A blind man miraculously receives the gift of his sight from Jesus; he is released from the darkness. Yet, in the light, he finds a tremendous challenge awaits him: the disbelief of others.

Jesus equates sight with sin; he equates blindness with sinlessness. He points out that those who judge the sight of others are blind themselves.

### CONSIDER
- Why can't the Pharisees accept the miracle?
- Besides sight, what other gifts did the blind man receive?

### LET US PRAY
- For the sight of faith and truth
- For all of us who suffer blindness in mind and heart
- For the perseverance to search for light in the midst of darkness
- For loving hearts that accept the miracles of others
- For our own personal intentions (shared with the group or held silently before the Lord)

## A REFLECTIVE MOMENT OF SILENCE

## ADDITIONAL ACTIVITIES/DISCUSSION
- What keeps people from seeing the power, peace, and love of Jesus in our society today?
- How are groups like ours often blind?

# Fifth Sunday in
# LENT

*"Lazarus, come out!"*
John 11:43

## WE GATHER IN PRAYER

Lord, draw us to yourself in death as well as in life. Steady our faith in the ultimate challenge: death. Give us the confidence to embrace your Son as both the light and the life.

We thank you, God, for the gift of your holy word. It instructs and inspires; it brings your life to our death...

### Amen

## READ JOHN 11:3-45

### REFLECT

Jesus' friend Lazarus is truly dead: four days dead! His body is in the tomb, and the natural process of decomposition has begun. Yet, Jesus' intimacy with God is so strong that even death is not an obstacle.

This incident is more than a return to life for a dead man. It is an opportunity for others to see and acknowledge Jesus as life itself.

### CONSIDER

■ Why is this gospel appropriate for the Lenten season?

■ Notice where this gospel is placed in the sequence of events. Why is this an appropriate place?

### LET US PRAY

■ For the deceased members of our families and those of us who continue to love them

■ For all those who harbor fear and uncertainty about life after death

■ For an appreciation of the communion of saints

■ For an honest longing to be happy with Jesus for all eternity

■ For our own personal intentions (shared with the group or held silently before the Lord)

### A REFLECTIVE MOMENT OF SILENCE

### ADDITIONAL ACTIVITIES/DISCUSSION

■ What does Lazarus symbolize for us in our faith journeys?

■ What personal friendships of our own call us into greater intimacy with Jesus?

(Palm Sunday)
# PASSION SUNDAY

*"...it must come to pass in this way..."*
Matthew 26:54

## WE GATHER IN PRAYER

Lord, bless us with a steady acceptance of your will. Like your Son, we want your will to be the directing force of our life choices.

Draw us to yourself, God, as you would have us come. Hold us steady along the way...

## Amen

## READ MATTHEW 26:14–27:66

### REFLECT

The final hours of Jesus' life are ticking away. The conspiracy to turn him over is arranged, the Passover meal is prepared and shared, and Jesus is arrested, tried, and executed. The gospel ends with Pilate giving orders for the grave to be sealed and guarded.

Jesus has many options during these final hours. He has the support of his followers, who will gladly arrange for his disappearance into the night. And as always, he has divine intervention. He relies on neither. He relies on the will of God.

### CONSIDER

- Why is this gospel read a week before Easter?
- What did Jesus accomplish by his crucifixion?

### LET US PRAY

- For the courage of Jesus, that we may follow God's will
- For the love of Jesus, that we may love at all cost
- For the spirit of Jesus, that we may face all challenges with faith
- For the humility of Jesus, that we may serve others
- For our own personal intentions (shared with the group or held silently before the Lord)

## A REFLECTIVE MOMENT OF SILENCE

## ADDITIONAL ACTIVITIES/DISCUSSION

- The story of Jesus is being lived out around the world today. Where and how?
- Would we like to pray the Way of the Cross as a group?

# The Season of EASTER

# EASTER SUNDAY

*...they did not yet understand...*
John 20:9

## WE GATHER IN PRAYER

Lord, instill in us a brilliant Easter faith. Show us how to search, discover, trust, and rejoice in the many mysteries of our faith.

Place in us an anticipation for the Coming of Christ and the resurrection of all...

### Amen

## READ JOHN 20:1-9

### REFLECT

Mary of Magdala goes to the tomb early in the morning. The account does not indicate why Mary goes to the tomb, but we can conjecture. She may have gone with her mourning, just as many return to the cemetery to "visit the grave" of a loved one. She may have intended to conduct certain burial rituals traditional in the Jewish faith.

Why Mary was at the tomb of her Lord is not particularly important. The fact is, she was there. Even in the face of death, she remained faithful to her Lord.

### CONSIDER

- Mary sees the stone removed; the disciples see the empty tomb. Compare and contrast these details.
- What model does Mary of Magdala offer us on our faith journeys today?

### LET US PRAY

- For joyful hearts this Easter season
- For the courage to share our Easter faith with others
- For the spiritual renewal of the universal Church
- For an acceptance of those mysteries of faith we cannot understand
- For our own personal intentions (shared with the group or held silently before the Lord)

### A REFLECTIVE MOMENT OF SILENCE

### ADDITIONAL ACTIVITIES/DISCUSSION

- What do we know about how Easter is observed in other countries?
- Let's reflect on our Lenten journey to see how it has enriched our joy this Easter.

# Second Sunday of
# EASTER

*"Peace be with you."*
John 20:19

## WE GATHER IN PRAYER

Lord, help us remember the connection between your death and your resurrection. Bless us with the gifts of your Spirit that allow us to know your presence in our midst, in our own dying and rising.

Renew our lives with Easter joy and peace, O God. Teach us to rejoice...

Amen

## READ JOHN 20:19-31

### REFLECT

Jesus enters into the midst of the disciples and extends peace. Immediately after that, he shows them the wounds in his hands and side. Jesus connects the importance of dying and rising to the experience of peace.

Jesus invites Thomas, the unbelieving disciple, to place his finger into the wounds. Notice that Scripture does not say that Thomas does, in fact, touch Jesus. Nonetheless, Thomas believes; he knows the peace Jesus offers.

### CONSIDER

- How is this incident significant to our faith?
- What connection is Jesus making between his wounds and his peace?

### LET US PRAY

- For the ability to communicate our faith to others
- For enthusiasm and zeal in sharing the Good News
- For a spirit of joy and peace
- For all those who struggle with the reality of Christ's presence in their midst
- For our own personal intentions (shared with the group or held silently before the Lord)

## A REFLECTIVE MOMENT OF SILENCE

## ADDITIONAL ACTIVITIES/DISCUSSION

- How can we become a more peace-filled and faith-filled community?
- Let's write a short prayer for greater faith; let's memorize it and repeat it often this week.

# Third Sunday of
# EASTER

*...they recognized him...*
Luke 24:31

## WE GATHER IN PRAYER

Lord, thank you for the opportunity to worship in liturgy, for your holy word, for your presence to us in the bread and wine. Help us to fully appreciate this wonder in our midst.

Instill in us a thirst for you, O God, a sacramental thirst...

# Amen

## READ LUKE 24:13-35

### REFLECT

This is perhaps the most beautiful of all appearance stories of Jesus. As two friends amble along trying to make sense of a major event in their lives, Jesus joins them. The three saunter on together, sharing conversation and camaraderie.

The key theme of the Emmaus story is the full portrayal of how Jesus continues to be present to us today: in community, in the sharing of the word, and in the breaking of the bread.

### CONSIDER

■ What role does the liturgy play in our faith lives?

■ Why is this a significant story to reflect on during the Easter season?

### LET US PRAY

■ For a love of Jesus present to us in the Eucharist

■ For a devotion to Jesus in the tabernacle

■ For a genuine joy of the risen Christ in our midst

■ For solidarity in Christ's Church

■ For our own personal intentions (shared with the group or held silently before the Lord)

### A REFLECTIVE MOMENT OF SILENCE

### ADDITIONAL ACTIVITIES/DISCUSSION

■ Who has been an Emmaus partner for us in living faithfully day to day?

■ Why is community important in the experience of faith?

# Fourth Sunday of
# EASTER

*"...the shepherd of the sheep."*
John 10:2

## WE GATHER IN PRAYER

Lord, we follow your Son, Jesus Christ. Teach us to know his voice amid the clatter and din of our daily lives. Show us how to follow the Good Shepherd.

As shepherds ourselves, crush our pride and instill in us your humility. Plant in our hearts a love for all people as we witness to your love...

Amen

## READ JOHN 10:1-10

### REFLECT

Jesus tries to show his listeners that he is the way to salvation. He uses the analogy of sheep and shepherd in an attempt to deliver his message directly and simply. His first attempt doesn't seem to be effective. "So Jesus said again..." (10:7).

Perhaps Jesus' second attempt is no more successful than his first, but it is different.

### CONSIDER
- How is Jesus' second attempt different from his first?
- How does this gospel support our Easter joy?

### LET US PRAY
- For all who search for happiness and peace
- For Christian unity
- For the ability to communicate the Good News with the love of a good shepherd
- For a strong and confident prayer life
- For our own personal intentions (shared with the group or held silently before the Lord)

## A REFLECTIVE MOMENT OF SILENCE

## ADDITIONAL ACTIVITIES/DISCUSSION
- How are we sheep? How are we shepherds?
- What are the special responsibilities of faithful shepherds?

# Fifth Sunday of
# EASTER

*"...how can we know the way?"*
John 14:5

## WE GATHER IN PRAYER

Lord, let us take comfort and reassurance in Jesus, your Son. Help us to trust in his promises of eternal life. Release us from doubt, untangle our confusions, and lighten our way.

Open our minds and hearts to Jesus' words...

Amen

## READ JOHN 14:1-12

### REFLECT

The scene is the upper room, the night of Jesus' trial. He feels an urgency to reassure his beloved friends, knowing that the ensuing hours are going to be terrifying for everyone. He speaks of preparing a place for them in his Father's house.

Thomas and Philip become our voices in that small gathering. "How can we know the way?" (14:5) and "Show us the Father" (14:8) are our questions and demands today.

### CONSIDER

■ Jesus says, "Do not let your hearts be troubled" (14:1). How do those words affect our belief in eternal life?

■ Jesus says, "...you know the way" (14:4). Do we?

### LET US PRAY

■ For all of us who are troubled in any way

■ For the peace of Christ, crucified and risen

■ For faithful patience under pressure

■ For the humility and courage to carry on Christ's mission

■ For our own personal intentions (shared with the group or held silently before the Lord)

### A REFLECTIVE MOMENT OF SILENCE

### ADDITIONAL ACTIVITIES/DISCUSSION

■ How do we know God more fully in knowing Jesus Christ?

■ How do our lives offer others a place to meet Jesus?

# Sixth Sunday of EASTER

*...the world will no longer see me..."*
John 14:19

## WE GATHER IN PRAYER

Lord, help us to hold confidently in our hearts a reverence for your commandments. Encourage us to seek your will in the details of our daily lives.

May our hearts be peaceful, O God, as we meditate on the full presence of Christ in our midst...

## Amen

## READ JOHN 14:15-21

## REFLECT

In the Sundays immediately following the Resurrection, the gospels focused on the risen Christ and his appearances. With Ascension only days away, the gospel now focuses on Jesus' departure and the indwelling of the Holy Spirit in the Church.

Jesus focuses on the importance of the commandments in the life of his followers. He makes a direct connection with following the commandments to loving him.

## CONSIDER

- What commandments is Jesus referring to when he says, "Whoever has my commandments and observes them is the one who loves me" (14:21)?
- Highlight those specific verses that refer to Jesus' Ascension.

## LET US PRAY

- For a reverence of all Jesus' teachings
- For a recognition of the Holy Spirit in our lives
- For all those who were welcomed into the Church at the Easter Vigil
- For ourselves, that we may carry the purpose of Christ's commandments foremost in our hearts
- For our own personal intentions (shared with the group or held silently before the Lord)

## A REFLECTIVE MOMENT OF SILENCE

## ADDITIONAL ACTIVITIES/DISCUSSION

- What good are commandments?
- How do we participate in the world's failure to accept the Spirit of truth that Jesus refers to (14:17)?

# ASCENSION OF THE LORD

*"Go, therefore..."*
Matthew 28:19

### WE GATHER IN PRAYER

Lord, inspire us to share the Good News, just as Jesus commissioned us to do. Build in us a conviction of your Son's abiding presence in our midst here and now.

Thank you for both the privilege and the responsibility to go into the world, to take your truth to the corners of the earth...

Amen

### READ MATTHEW 28:16-20

### REFLECT

Jesus is risen and arranges to meet his disciples in Galilee. At the gathering, there is a mixed response of worship and doubt. How familiar that sounds to us today in our own experiences of faith.

Although Matthew does not specifically mention the Ascension as an event, he clearly implies some kind of departure and a commissioning of the disciples to "carry on."

### CONSIDER
- Why was there a mixture of faith and doubt expressed by the disciples at this meeting with Jesus?
- What are the three parts of the commission Jesus gave his disciples?

### LET US PRAY
- For a firm and faithful conviction in the risen Lord
- For the courage to share our faith with those who do not embrace the Christian tradition
- For an understanding of our baptismal vows
- For all those who find no joy in their experience of Christianity
- For our own personal intentions (shared with the group or held silently before the Lord)

### A REFLECTIVE MOMENT OF SILENCE

### ADDITIONAL ACTIVITIES/DISCUSSION
- Let's review our baptismal vows and discuss what they mean in living our faith day to day.
- How do we live the three-part commission that Jesus left all of us?

# Seventh Sunday of

# EASTER

*"Everything of mine is yours...everything of yours is mine..."*
John 17:10

## WE GATHER IN PRAYER

Lord, thank you for the privilege to be with Jesus in prayer. Plant in us open hearts that are willing to be as intimate with you as your Son was.

O God, may all our thoughts, words, and deeds praise you in every way...

Amen

## READ JOHN 17:1-11

### REFLECT

This Scripture passage continues to celebrate the Easter season. We reflect on Jesus' farewell prayer offered to God in the midst of his followers. We are privileged to see the intimacy he shares with his Father.

We notice how broad Jesus' prayer is. He praises God's splendor, he prays for himself, and he prays for his friends. In this intense connection with his Father, Jesus offers us a fine model of prayer.

### CONSIDER

- What about this Scripture passage is passionately unique?
- Why is this Scripture passage a model for our own prayer?

### LET US PRAY

- For the perseverance to develop our personal prayer life
- For an appreciation of God's wonder in nature
- For the kingdom in our midst
- For a greater love of Scripture
- For our own personal intentions (shared with the group or held silently before the Lord)

### A REFLECTIVE MOMENT OF SILENCE

### ADDITIONAL ACTIVITIES/DISCUSSION

- How do we feel when we hear others pray for us?
- As a group, let's try to write a prayer that captures the same intimacy and passion with which Jesus prayed.

# PENTECOST

### WE GATHER IN PRAYER

Lord, break open your peace in our midst. Let us find your goodness waiting for us in every minute of every day.

Empower us, O God, to carry your peace into our daily lives. Draw us to yourself and allow us to be your light to the world...

## Amen

### READ JOHN 20:19-23

#### REFLECT

Pentecost means fifty; it is fifty days since we celebrated Jesus' Resurrection. It is ten days since we celebrated Jesus' Ascension.

The Scripture rings of peace: Jesus bringing his peace into the fearful hearts of his followers. Today, Jesus continues to bring his peace into our hearts. Although Pentecost is often considered the birthday of the Church, we can know the joy of Pentecost every day, again and again.

#### CONSIDER
- What was the mental and spiritual state of the disciples prior to Jesus' appearance in their midst?
- What significance does this passage have to our faith journeys?

#### LET US PRAY
- For an appreciation of God's true presence in the Church
- For the courage to live Pentecost in our daily lives
- For the ability to articulate the teachings of Jesus and his Church
- For the power of the Spirit to saturate the teaching authority of the Church
- For our own personal intentions (shared with the group or held silently before the Lord)

### A REFLECTIVE MOMENT OF SILENCE

### ADDITIONAL ACTIVITIES/DISCUSSION
- Why is forgiveness an important dimension of the Christian experience?
- Let's share the name we took at confirmation and explain why we selected that name.

# The Season of
# ORDINARY TIME

# TRINITY SUNDAY

*For God so loved the world...*
John 3:16

## WE GATHER IN PRAYER

God, thank you for loving us so deeply and completely and perfectly. Thank you for filling our lives with the beauty of your creation, the love of your Son, and the power of your Spirit.

Come to us in the mystery of your trinitarian nature and teach us to rejoice in that mystery...

### Amen

## READ JOHN 3:16-18

### REFLECT

This brief gospel is couched in the account of Nicodemus coming to Jesus under cover of night. Drawn by the wonders he had witnessed and the power of God stirring his heart, Nicodemus responds—albeit cautiously and somewhat skeptically.

Nicodemus is perplexed by Jesus' words about being born again because he takes Jesus literally. But Jesus is talking about the birth of a soul into the full life of God: God the Father, God the Son, and God the Holy Spirit.

### CONSIDER

■ Why does Jesus speak figuratively here instead of literally?

■ How is Nicodemus a faith model for us today?

### LET US PRAY

■ For the grace to follow Jesus

■ For the grace to seek first the kingdom of God in all the decisions we make

■ For a sincere reverence of the Holy Trinity

■ For the humility to allow mystery a role in our faith experience

■ For our own personal intentions (shared with the group or held silently before the Lord)

### A REFLECTIVE MOMENT OF SILENCE

### ADDITIONAL ACTIVITIES/DISCUSSION

■ Let's think of symbols and actions that reflect our belief in the triune God.

■ How would we explain the Trinity to a person inquiring about the faith?

# BODY AND BLOOD OF CHRIST

*"...the one who feeds on me..."*
John 6:57

## WE GATHER IN PRAYER

Lord, thank you for the precious gift of Eucharist, a perfect union with Jesus, your Son. May we be truly humble in our awareness of this gift—and truly joyful.

Nourish us in the prayer of the Mass, O God. Nourish us in the community, in your holy word, and in the body and blood of Jesus...

Amen

## READ JOHN 6:51-58

### REFLECT

Jesus makes a statement that his listeners can hardly believe: "...the bread that I will give is my flesh..." (6:51). The quarreling Jews surely had mental images akin to cannibalism.

Today, we know the meaning of Jesus' words. We have welcomed Jesus into our hearts countless times in the Eucharist. We know the sustaining grace that is ours in Communion.

### CONSIDER

- If we had been present listening to Jesus, how might we have responded to his comment?
- Why would the Jews have quarreled among themselves?

### LET US PRAY

- For a strong faith in and joyful reverence of the Eucharist
- For all children preparing to celebrate their first Communion
- For all those who feel alienated from the Church and the sacramental life it offers
- For ourselves, when we know our faith to be faint
- For our own personal intentions (shared with the group or held silently before the Lord)

### A REFLECTIVE MOMENT OF SILENCE

### ADDITIONAL ACTIVITIES/DISCUSSION

- How might the shortage of priests to celebrate the Eucharist affect our faith?
- Why would the Church designate a special feast for the body and blood of Christ?

# Second Sunday in
# ORDINARY TIME

*John testified further...*
John 1:32

## WE GATHER IN PRAYER

Lord, plant in us the same wisdom that John the Baptist displayed when he recognized Jesus, the Son of God. Open our eyes to see and open our hearts to speak of the One who takes away the sin of the world.

Let our thoughts and words speak of Jesus, that everyone we meet will know we are Christians by our love...

## Amen

## READ JOHN 1:29-34

## REFLECT

All four evangelists—John, Matthew, Luke, and Mark—mention Jesus' baptism. John's gospel differs from the others, however, in that it is less of a detailed account and more of a symbolic declaration.

John the Baptist recognizes Jesus. He has remained loyal to his calling, to bear witness to the Lamb of God. He does not fail.

## CONSIDER

- How does this account of Jesus' baptism differ from the other gospels? (See Matthew 3:13-17, Mark 1:9-11, and Luke 3:21-22.)
- How does John the Baptist remain loyal to his calling?

## LET US PRAY

- For those who have never heard the Good News
- For those who have heard the Good News but are frightened by it
- For the spiritual maturity to witness to Christ at home, at school, at work
- For the ability to articulate the teachings of Jesus
- For our own personal intentions (shared with the group or held silently before the Lord)

## A REFLECTIVE MOMENT OF SILENCE

## ADDITIONAL ACTIVITIES/DISCUSSION

- Let's invite someone who has been to the Holy Land to share his or her experiences with us.
- What are our greatest challenges to witnessing to Jesus today?

# Third Sunday in
# ORDINARY TIME

*...they left their nets...*
Matthew 4:20

## WE GATHER IN PRAYER

Lord, open the ears of our souls to hear Jesus' call and to respond to his invitation to join his disciples. Fill us with the grace to take the love of Jesus into our daily lives.

Show us, O God, how to call to others. Train our hearts to speak of Jesus' unconditional love where it is most needed...

## Amen

## READ MATTHEW 4:12-23

### REFLECT

Jesus travels north to Capernaum, a town along the Sea of Galilee. Capernaum is a crossroad for commerce. While there, Jesus hears that John has been arrested. Perhaps as a result of that, and because Capernaum is a major gathering point, Jesus uses John's words to launch his ministry: "Repent, for the kingdom of heaven is at hand" (4:17).

Jesus preaches his clear and simple message: "Be sorry for your sins because the kingdom of God is at hand." To some individuals, like Simon (Peter), Andrew, James, and John, he extends a direct invitation: "Come after me..." (4:19).

### CONSIDER
- Why would Jesus begin teaching after receiving the news of John's imprisonment?
- What is the significance of this gospel to our own personal faith journeys?

### LET US PRAY
- For open-mindedness
- For the willingness to change our lives as the invitation of Jesus fills our hearts
- For all world leaders, that a passion for gospel values will guide their choices
- For ourselves, that regularly sharing prayer and Scripture will strengthen our faith
- For our own personal intentions (shared with the group or held silently before the Lord)

## A REFLECTIVE MOMENT OF SILENCE

## ADDITIONAL ACTIVITIES/DISCUSSION
- How does the invitation of Jesus cause tension in families? at work? in society?
- What all is involved in "repentance"?

# Fourth Sunday in
# ORDINARY TIME

*...your reward will be great...*
Matthew 5:12

## WE GATHER IN PRAYER

Lord, direct our hearts to seek what is really worthwhile in life: the life of your Spirit. Show us how to discern kingdom goodness from what society labels "good."

Claim our attention, O God, and soften our hearts to the needs of the poor...

**Amen**

## READ MATTHEW 5:1-12

### REFLECT

If you are asked, "For whom was Jesus most concerned?" you would likely respond, "The poor." It seems Jesus keeps the poor ever in front of us. It is no casual incident that he mentions the poor first in his directives for life.

"Blessed are the poor in spirit..." (5:3) can refer to those who lack basic human comforts and necessities. It can also refer to those who are poor in the claims they make on life, those who need nothing and want nothing, only the love of God.

### CONSIDER

How are each of the following poor?
- ...the mournful and the meek
- ...those who hunger and thirst for righteousness
- ...the merciful
- ...the clean of heart
- ...the peacemakers
- ...those who are persecuted for the sake of righteousness

## LET US PRAY

- For the poor, that they will know relief
- For ourselves, that we may recognize the poor
- For our enemies and those people we simply don't like
- For those who search for happiness in shallow things
- For our own personal intentions (shared with the group or held silently before the Lord)

## A REFLECTIVE MOMENT OF SILENCE

## ADDITIONAL ACTIVITIES/DISCUSSION

- What can we do as a group to assist the poor in our area?
- How do we live the beatitudes in our daily lives?

# Fifth Sunday in
# ORDINARY TIME

*"...the salt of the earth."*
Matthew 5:13

## WE GATHER IN PRAYER

Lord, thank you for the many opportunities we have to influence the lives of others. When we fail to see these opportunities, open our eyes; show us the way.

Grant that we will be a source of courage and inspiration to one another...

## Amen

## READ MATTHEW 5:13-16

### REFLECT

Jesus uses the common substance of salt to explain the influence his followers can have in the lives of others. He uses the simple appliance of a lamp to make the same point. He points out that it makes no sense to turn on the light switch and then cover the lamp with a blanket.

Jesus tries to inspire his listeners to have confidence in their own faith. In his use of simple things, like salt and light, he urges his followers to make a difference, even a little difference.

### CONSIDER
- Why is this gospel positioned after the Sermon on the Mount?
- Why does Jesus stress the importance of others seeing "your good deeds" (5:16)?

### LET US PRAY
- For all those who wield a great deal of influence in society
- For those who communicate Christ's words in formal educational settings
- For the spirit to be salt; for the wisdom to be light
- For those who do not think their efforts will make a difference
- For our own personal intentions (shared with the group or held silently before the Lord)

### A REFLECTIVE MOMENT OF SILENCE

### ADDITIONAL ACTIVITIES/DISCUSSION
- Let's look at one granule of salt and ponder how one small particle like that can make a difference.
- What other symbols represent people who are influential? Can we adopt one of those symbols?

# Sixth Sunday in
# ORDINARY TIME

*"...I say to you..."*
Matthew 5:22

## WE GATHER IN PRAYER

Lord, help us understand your teachings. Give us a passion to pore over your word, to ponder its significance, to respect its challenge.

Build in us a confidence for the ancient wisdom of Jesus that remains relevant to life today...

# Amen

## READ MATTHEW 5:17-37

### REFLECT

There is a distinct pattern to this reading that is hard to overlook. Generally, it sounds like Jesus is saying, "You have heard....But now this is what I say." Jesus puts his comments into the context of law and assures his followers that he has not come "to abolish but to fulfill" it (5:17).

Jesus is emphasizing the importance of the Spirit of the law, the part of the law that is central to the life of faith. The follower of Jesus will internalize the law, going beyond the specific dos and don'ts that the law specifies.

### CONSIDER

■ Pinpoint each law Jesus discusses and note where he places the focus.

■ Why does this gospel follow the passage about being the salt of the earth?

### LET US PRAY

■ For a true friendship with Jesus

■ For those of us who lose sight of the Spirit of the law

■ For compassion and patience

■ For all those who make and enforce laws

■ For our own personal intentions (shared with the group or held silently before the Lord)

### A REFLECTIVE MOMENT OF SILENCE

### ADDITIONAL ACTIVITIES/DISCUSSION

■ What is the spirit of all civil law?

■ What is the spirit of the Ten Commandments?

# Seventh Sunday in
# ORDINARY TIME

*"...offer no resistance..."*
Matthew 5:39

## WE GATHER IN PRAYER

Lord, instill in us the wisdom to know what love means. Teach us to love everyone in your name, to love those who are difficult to love.

Soften our hearts and take from us any desire to get even with others, to issue our own justice...

Amen

## READ MATTHEW 5:38-48

### REFLECT

There was an old law that stated, "An eye for an eye and a tooth for a tooth." This law put limits on retaliation; the harm done was somehow offset by an equally harmful thing being done to the perpetrator.

Jesus explains that this law is lacking. Those who are serious about the teachings of Jesus will not return an eye for an eye and a tooth for a tooth; Christians will go the "extra mile."

### CONSIDER

- Does Jesus mean that we should take all injustices in a passive manner?
- What specific challenges to the Christian way of life are presented in this gospel?

### LET US PRAY

- For a better of understanding of love and forgiveness
- For all those we love to hate
- For those we do not love fully
- For a spirit of kindness and justice at home and at work
- For our own personal intentions (shared with the group or held silently before the Lord)

## A REFLECTIVE MOMENT OF SILENCE

## ADDITIONAL ACTIVITIES/DISCUSSION

- How does the lesson of this gospel make for good, healthy living?
- Who are our neighbors? our enemies? Who persecutes us?

# Eighth Sunday in
# ORDINARY TIME

*"...do not worry..."*
Matthew 6:25

## WE GATHER IN PRAYER

Lord, thank you for the wisdom of your word. Bless us with an understanding of service and loyalty. Teach us to appreciate without clinging, to respect without claiming.

Direct our feet on the path that leads to your kingdom. Fill our hearts with delight in serving you...

# Amen

## READ MATTHEW 6:24-34

### REFLECT

Our culture refers to those who seem to have a handle on life as people who "have it all together." Jesus speaks in similar terms. We are blessed when we see that God comes first in everything.

Jesus teaches that it is senseless to be anxious. Anxiety has no place in the heart of a disciple of Christ who has learned to trust in God's love and mercy.

### CONSIDER

■ Which sentence in this Scripture summarizes Jesus' whole message?

■ Jesus says, "Do not worry about tomorrow" (6:34). Are we to take these words literally?

### LET US PRAY

■ For ourselves and our great need to feel secure

■ For a true dedication and faith in Jesus Christ

■ For the wisdom to prioritize with Jesus' message as our rule of thumb

■ For a genuinely grateful heart

■ For our own personal intentions (shared with the group or held silently before the Lord)

## A REFLECTIVE MOMENT OF SILENCE

## ADDITIONAL ACTIVITIES/DISCUSSION

■ We worry. How can we justify our worry by gospel values—or can we?

■ Let's write a prayer that places all our concerns into God's hands.

# Ninth Sunday in
# ORDINARY TIME

*"...the will of my Father..."*
Matthew 7:21

## WE GATHER IN PRAYER

Lord, release our hearts and minds from routine. Enkindle in us an acute sense of being alive in your love, of embracing your name and your will with a conscientious attention.

Come, Holy Spirit. Help us build a faith on solid ground...

# Amen

## READ MATTHEW 7:21-27

### REFLECT

Jesus uses a parable to illustrate how necessary it is to do the will of God. If we hear God's word and follow it, we build our lives on a solid foundation.

On the other hand, if we hear God's word and do not put it into practice, our lives' foundation is shaky, to say the least. The difficulties of life become greater threats.

### CONSIDER
- How do we know the will of God?
- What does Jesus mean when he says, "I never knew you" (7:23)?

### LET US PRAY
- For those who cling to fantasies, that they may find the courage to face reality
- For those who suffer persecution for justice's sake
- For the courage to set a good Christian example by aligning our faith and our deeds
- For faith in a God who knows our needs even before we know them
- For our own personal intentions (shared with the group or held silently before the Lord)

## A REFLECTIVE MOMENT OF SILENCE

## ADDITIONAL ACTIVITIES/DISCUSSION
- Let's look at how we actually build a little on solid ground—and a little on sand.
- What is wisdom?

# Tenth Sunday in
# ORDINARY TIME

*"...tax collectors and sinners..."*
Matthew 9:10

## WE GATHER IN PRAYER

Lord, fill our hearts with genuine compassion to respond to all people as your precious creatures. Melt our hearts with your grace.

Help us to be honest with ourselves and others and to see that we are all one in the heart of the God who made us...

Amen

## READ MATTHEW 9:9-13

### REFLECT

Being a tax collector meant being on the inside of the Roman law. It did not mean being on the inside of the Jewish law. The Romans, the conquerors of the Jews, employed Jews to collect taxes from their own people.

Naturally, the Jewish people had little patience and no respect for their own who were tax collectors. They were classified as sinners, as impure—and it is one of these that Jesus personally invites to join him.

### CONSIDER

- What does Jesus mean when he says, "I did not come to call the righteous but sinners" (9:13)?
- What is the significance of this Scripture to our overall faith journeys?

### LET US PRAY

- For all those who hold public office
- For open hearts, free of judgmentalism
- For the gift of genuine hospitality
- For the gift of mercy
- For our own personal intentions (shared with the group or held silently before the Lord)

## A REFLECTIVE MOMENT OF SILENCE

## ADDITIONAL ACTIVITIES/DISCUSSION

- How do we extend mercy? How do we receive mercy?
- How is Christianity basically countercultural?

# Eleventh Sunday in
# ORDINARY TIME

*"As you go..."*
Matthew 10:7

## WE GATHER IN PRAYER

Lord, renew us in the name of Jesus for the journey of faith that is our entire life. Bless us in ways that enable us to bless, heal, and care for others.

We want to be compassionate and trusting in the love of Jesus, your Son...

## Amen

## READ MATTHEW 9:36–10:8

### REFLECT

Notice how the evangelist is specific about who is called; there's no doubt about who was part of this band. Granted the privilege of miracles, Jesus sends those who are called into the field to reap a harvest.

In addition to being specific about who is sent, the evangelist is specific about what is expected of the twelve: cure the sick, raise the dead, cleanse lepers, drive out demons. The apostles know exactly what to do.

### CONSIDER

- What might have been Matthew's reasons for listing the names of the twelve apostles?
- Jesus says that the harvest is abundant. Is it? If yes, in what way? If no, why not?

### LET US PRAY

- For all those who feel lost along their journey of faith
- For an understanding of evangelization
- For all those who labor with love in the harvest of souls
- For alert hearts that hear God's call
- For our own personal intentions (shared with the group or held silently before the Lord)

### A REFLECTIVE MOMENT OF SILENCE

### ADDITIONAL ACTIVITIES/DISCUSSION

- What experiences have we had of "harvesters" being less than Christian?
- Jesus says that without cost we have received and without cost we are to give. What does this mean to us today?

# Twelfth Sunday in
# ORDINARY TIME

*"...the hairs of your head are counted."*
Matthew 10:30

## WE GATHER IN PRAYER

Lord, lift the heavy burden of fear from our hearts. In the face of harassment and ridicule, arm our souls with your steady presence.

Quiet our insecurities, bless our timidity, move our hearts toward trust...

## Amen

## READ MATTHEW 10:26-33

### REFLECT

This Scripture continues the commissioning of the apostles. (See last week's gospel.) Jesus is trying to build the apostles' confidence in the God who loves them, who protects them. He is trying to tell them that they will, indeed, know fear—but that their fear will not destroy them.

The fact that God has counted every hair of our head is a profound example of God's personal investment in and intimacy with each of us.

### CONSIDER

■ How much courage would the apostles have taken from these words of Jesus?

■ What does the word *deny* mean as it is used in this Scripture passage?

### LET US PRAY

■ For those who are persecuted for their faith

■ For those of us who are fearful and timid

■ For a greater understanding of our own faith

■ For the ability to articulate our faith

■ For our own personal intentions (shared with the group or held silently before the Lord)

### A REFLECTIVE MOMENT OF SILENCE

### ADDITIONAL ACTIVITIES/DISCUSSION

■ Would we find Jesus' words especially supportive today in times of crisis or danger?

■ Let's share some of our personal experiences of intense intimacy with God.

# Thirteenth Sunday in
# ORDINARY TIME

*"...for my sake..."*
Matthew 10:39

## WE GATHER IN PRAYER

Lord, renew our hearts as followers of your Son, Jesus Christ. Instill in us a courage to face the unique challenges that come to us as followers of Jesus and communicators of the Good News.

Help us to adjust our priorities to align with gospel values...

## Amen

## READ MATTHEW 10:37-42

## REFLECT

Jesus is giving instruction to his disciples. They are going to be communicating the gospel. They will meet opposition. In fact, Jesus suggests that the opposition might even come from their own family members.

Jesus is God's Good News, sent for our salvation. Many acknowledge that fact but do not arrange their lives to reflect their belief.

## CONSIDER

- This is the end of a long set of instructions that Jesus gave his apostles. How might the apostles be feeling by this time?
- How much of this reading should we take literally?

## LET US PRAY

- For the courage to follow Christ
- For the grace to witness to Christ in our words and actions
- For harmonious relationships within families
- For the grace to respect the religious convictions of others
- For our own personal intentions (shared with the group or held silently before the Lord)

## A REFLECTIVE MOMENT OF SILENCE

## ADDITIONAL ACTIVITIES/DISCUSSION

- What does it mean to "receive" someone?
- Is the idea of reward part of our faith journeys? If yes, how? If no, why not?

# Fourteenth Sunday in
# ORDINARY TIME

*"Come to me..."*
Matthew 11:28

## WE GATHER IN PRAYER

Lord, we focus on your invitation to come to you, to take our rest in you, to take your yoke upon ourselves. Draw us to yourself by intensifying that invitation in our hearts.

Teach us to be childlike in our faith, to trust with playful abandon...

*Amen*

## READ MATTHEW 11:25-30

### REFLECT

Jesus seems to be saying that the learned and the clever are not well-disposed to know God's revelation. The Pharisees and religious leaders of Jesus' day are well-versed in the Mosaic Law, yet they're unable to grasp God's revelation in their midst: Jesus.

Jesus encourages his listeners to come to him, to rest with him and in him. He says that with him, burdens are lightened.

### CONSIDER

■ Who are the childlike that Jesus refers to?

■ How does this Scripture show Jesus as having a deep-rooted understanding of himself?

### LET US PRAY

■ For the gift of understanding

■ For sincere hearts, well-disposed for conversion

■ For humility, meekness, and joy

■ For educators and those commissioned as the "teaching authority of the Church"

■ For our own personal intentions (shared with the group or held silently before the Lord)

### A REFLECTIVE MOMENT OF SILENCE

### ADDITIONAL ACTIVITIES/DISCUSSION

■ How have our own daily burdens been lightened because of our faith in Jesus Christ?

■ What is the difference between being "childlike" and being "childish"?

# Fifteenth Sunday in ORDINARY TIME

*...he spoke to them...*
Matthew 13:3

## WE GATHER IN PRAYER

Lord, when your Son speaks to us, open our hearts to hear. Make us eager and thirsty for what he has to say.

May we be sowers of your word, O God, and may we also be the good soil onto which the word falls...

Amen

## READ MATTHEW 13:1-9

## REFLECT

This gospel describes a peaceful setting. Jesus comes out of the house and sits by the beautiful seashore, only to move into a boat as the crowd gathers. With love and compassion, Jesus looks into the eager faces of his listeners.

Jesus teaches in a way that is easy to understand: he uses a story. Yet, it's more than a story; it's a parable. Jesus uses familiar settings, people, and actions to tell a story that points to a deeper truth of faith.

## CONSIDER
- What is Jesus suggesting when he says, "Whoever has ears ought to hear" (13:9)?
- What parallel can we define for each kind of soil mentioned in the Scripture reading?

## LET US PRAY
- For perseverance
- For those times when we are the path, rocky ground, shallow soil, and thorns
- For those of us who struggle with addictions and compulsive behavior
- For all those who are interested in becoming Catholic
- For our own personal intentions (shared with the group or held silently before the Lord)

## A REFLECTIVE MOMENT OF SILENCE

## ADDITIONAL ACTIVITIES/DISCUSSION
- Let's retell this parable with imagery other than sowing.
- How do we experience the word of God bearing fruit as a result of our meeting every week?

# Sixteenth Sunday in
# ORDINARY TIME

*"...tie them in bundles for burning..."*
Matthew 13:30

## WE GATHER IN PRAYER

Lord, thank you for the good and the bad times that constitute life. We draw on your strength to endure, and we trust in your providence.

Alert us, O God, to those influences that creep in like weeds to entangle our lives of faith...

## Amen

## READ MATTHEW 13:24-30

### REFLECT

Jesus tells another parable. This one, like last week, is also about sowing seeds. According to the gospel, the slaves of the household are fairly dismayed. They immediately identify an enemy's hand in the whole thing, and then they want to root out the weeds.

The master, however, is wise. He knows that pulling the weeds may weaken or destroy the wheat. He suggests a way to "harvest" the goodness of the wheat (gather it into the barn) and "harvest" the goodness of the weeds (use them for fuel).

### CONSIDER

■ Who does the master represent in this parable? Who do the slaves represent? What does the wheat represent? What do the weeds represent?

■ Jesus suggests that there is an advantage to letting the wheat and the weeds grow together. What is that advantage?

### LET US PRAY

■ For the gift of the Holy Spirit that helps us discern wisely and faithfully

■ For the wisdom to stay in the struggle with the weeds of life

■ For the joy of Christ to guide our faith journeys

■ For all those who teach and guide

■ For our own personal intentions (shared with the group or held silently before the Lord)

### A REFLECTIVE MOMENT OF SILENCE

### ADDITIONAL ACTIVITIES/DISCUSSION

■ What kind of influences undermine the Good News in our own personal lives?

■ When have we allowed a misfortune to become an opportunity for God to work a wonder?

# Seventeenth Sunday in
# ORDINARY TIME

*"...both the new and the old...."*
Matthew 13:52

## WE GATHER IN PRAYER

Lord, impress on our hearts a genuine respect for the treasures of your kingdom. Give us insights into all that is truly your goodness.

Let nothing distract us from perfect union with you, O God. Clear our vision, that we may claim you as our pearl of great price...

## Amen

## READ MATTHEW 13:44-52

### REFLECT

This is another "story." Jesus uses this parable to impress on his listeners the real value of the Good News. Notice that the farmer finds a treasure in the field; he wasn't looking for it. He simply came across it in his daily work.

Notice, too, that the merchant is going about his daily work as well, which happens to be looking for valuable treasures. Both the farmer and the merchant, although differently oriented, find the treasure, sell everything, and buy it.

### CONSIDER

- Is Jesus suggesting that we sell everything we have for the sake of heaven?
- If Jesus asked us "Do you understand all these things?" (13:51) what would be our reply?

### LET US PRAY

- For a genuine love of God
- For a desire that focuses on the true treasures of life
- For the wisdom to know the treasures of heaven that are in our midst
- For a strong will in choosing what leads to the kingdom of heaven
- For our own personal intentions (shared with the group or held silently before the Lord)

### A REFLECTIVE MOMENT OF SILENCE

### ADDITIONAL ACTIVITIES/DISCUSSION

- How can we seek the treasures of heaven while being responsible to our families?
- Let's each identify one thing that we would find difficult to let go of—even for the kingdom of heaven.

# Eighteenth Sunday in
# ORDINARY TIME

*...fragments left over...*
Matthew 14:20

## WE GATHER IN PRAYER

Lord, there are fragments of your goodness scattered throughout our days. Open our eyes to taste of your constant goodness, to see your miracles in our midst.

Refresh our hearts with generosity, O God, that we may feed others with your truth...

Amen

## READ MATTHEW 14:13-21

### REFLECT

John the Baptist has just been executed, and Jesus wants to be alone with his sadness. But the crowds press in on him—and he does not ignore them. He gives them the nourishment of his words, and he nourishes their bodies.

When we encounter Jesus, we will always find that there is not only "enough" but also "more than enough." Just as the disciples realized, we will always have plenty left over when we share the Good News.

### CONSIDER

■ Is there a way to destroy the mystery of this Scripture with a logical explanation? What would that explanation be?

■ What is the significance of "leftovers" in this Scripture?

### LET US PRAY

■ For those who never have enough, let alone leftovers

■ For the homeless

■ For our own poverty of heart and spirit

■ For a deep appreciation of the Real Presence of Christ in the Eucharist

■ For our own personal intentions (shared with the group or held silently before the Lord)

### A REFLECTIVE MOMENT OF SILENCE

### ADDITIONAL ACTIVITIES/DISCUSSION

■ Where is there "surplus" in our own lives? What do we do with that surplus?

■ How does this Scripture speak to environmental issues?

# Nineteenth Sunday in
# ORDINARY TIME

*"...if it is you..."*
Matthew 14:28

## WE GATHER IN PRAYER

Lord, steady our gaze on you. When the storms of life pound against us on all sides, hold our gaze of faith steady on your love.

Bless us all with a sound faith in your power and strength...

## Amen

## READ MATTHEW 14:22-33

### REFLECT

How many times have we heard ourselves and others say, "I can't believe it." We usually do believe, it's just that we're so excited. This is Peter's reaction: "I can't believe it."

Peter acts on his faith and steps out of the boat to approach Jesus. In the midst of a powerful moment of faith, however, Peter doubts. Simultaneously, he knows faith—and he knows doubt.

### CONSIDER

■ What does Jesus do the moment Peter doubts? How is this action significant?

■ Is Peter a man of little faith or of great faith?

### LET US PRAY

■ For all those who seek God with a sincere heart

■ For a belief in miracles

■ For a strong faith with or without miracles

■ For our faith community

■ For our own personal intentions (shared with the group or held silently before the Lord)

### A REFLECTIVE MOMENT OF SILENCE

### ADDITIONAL ACTIVITIES/DISCUSSION

■ Let's write a litany of the things we believe in faith—yet doubt.

■ How do we display our faith in God by reaching out to others in our own neediness?

# Twentieth Sunday in
# ORDINARY TIME

*"...great is your faith!"*
Matthew 15:28

## WE GATHER IN PRAYER

God, soften our hearts. Coat us with a mantle of compassion and humility. Fill our hearts with a faith in you that knows no boundaries, no limits.

Help us comprehend your graciousness and generosity, O God...

## Amen

## READ MATTHEW 15:21-28

### REFLECT

The Canaanite woman in the gospel story is not a Jew. She is an outsider. Jesus' mission, as he tries to tell the woman, is first to Israel.

Jesus' reference to dogs applies to Gentiles, those outside the Chosen People of Yahweh. With the woman's persistence and display of great faith, Jesus responds.

### CONSIDER

■ If Jesus is such a loving and compassionate person, why does he initially refuse to consider this woman's needs?

■ What significance does this Scripture have on our own experience of faith?

### LET US PRAY

■ For a greater understanding of Scripture

■ For a deeper faith

■ For those who mourn without the support of faith

■ For the gifts of piety and perseverance

■ For our own personal intentions (shared with the group or held silently before the Lord)

### A REFLECTIVE MOMENT OF SILENCE

### ADDITIONAL ACTIVITIES/DISCUSSION

■ Let's make a list of our prayer priorities and concentrate on these as a group this week.

■ What if our prayers aren't answered?

# Twenty-First Sunday in
# ORDINARY TIME

*"You are the Messiah..."*
Matthew 16:16

## WE GATHER IN PRAYER

Lord, we ask that you open our hearts to see your goodness and glory. Humbly, we acknowledge our blindness and pray for the insight of Peter.

Hold the eyes of our souls on you, O Lord, that we may announce to the world, "Jesus is, indeed, the Messiah"...

## Amen

## READ MATTHEW 16:13-20

### REFLECT

More and more people are learning about Jesus. As they hear about his miracles, his popularity increases. He becomes a major public figure. His name begins to come up in daily conversation.

Jesus asks his disciples who people think he is. The disciples say that people aren't sure. They express views that Jesus is one of the prophets, Jeremiah, or Elijah. They even suggest that he is John the Baptist. It is Peter who identifies Jesus as the Messiah.

### CONSIDER

- Why does Jesus put his disciples through this exercise of identity?
- How is this Scripture relevant to our own faith journeys?

### LET US PRAY

- For families in our parish who do not feel a full sense of community
- For those who doubt the identity of Jesus
- For the Holy Spirit's gift of piety
- For an appreciation of the guidance God gives in the teaching authority of the Church
- For our own personal intentions (shared with the group or held silently before the Lord)

### A REFLECTIVE MOMENT OF SILENCE

### ADDITIONAL ACTIVITIES/DISCUSSION

- Let's invite someone to teach us about the difference between Church doctrine, Church teaching, and tradition.
- How does the presence of the Holy Father influence our daily faith journeys?

# Twenty-Second Sunday in

# ORDINARY TIME

*"...for my sake..."*
Matthew 16:25

## WE GATHER IN PRAYER

Lord, bless us with the courage to face our own individual life crosses. Be our rock of faith when sacrifice is demanded of us.

Allow us, O God, to walk our path of faith, not out of fear but for love, for your sake...

## Amen

## READ MATTHEW 16:21-27

### REFLECT

When Jesus explains to his disciples that he has to go to Jerusalem where he will be put to death, they can hardly believe what they hear. Peter has just declared that Jesus is the long-awaited Messiah.

So, Peter protests—and Jesus points out that Peter's resistance is a hindrance to God's plan. Jesus goes on to explain that belief in him will undoubtedly mean great sacrifice.

### CONSIDER

■ How is Peter a stumbling block to God's plan?

■ Why is "...for my sake..." (16:25) a critical phrase in this Scripture?

## LET US PRAY

■ For all those who suffer in any way because of their Christian faith

■ For all those who suffer the influence of peer pressure

■ For an understanding of what it means to be a true Christian

■ For the Holy Spirit's gift of courage

■ For our own personal intentions (shared with the group or held silently before the Lord)

## A REFLECTIVE MOMENT OF SILENCE

## ADDITIONAL ACTIVITIES/DISCUSSION

■ How are we like Peter?

■ How have we lost our lives for Jesus' sake?

# Twenty-Third Sunday in
# ORDINARY TIME

*"...where two or three are gathered..."*
Matthew 18:20

## WE GATHER IN PRAYER

Lord, help us better understand the meaning of community, the privileges of being part of a faith community, the responsibilities of being part of a faith community.

Fill our hearts with compassion; pull the strangling fingers of judgmentalism from our minds...

### Amen

## READ MATTHEW 18:15-20

### REFLECT

Jesus is concerned about reconciling those who are not in harmony. He longs for friendship and fellowship among his followers.

His direction in this gospel selection appears to relate to some public sin. First, individuals attempt to resolve their differences between themselves. Others are involved in the process when a one-on-one approach fails. Jesus is highlighting a crucial ingredient in the life of a healthy community.

### CONSIDER

■ What does Jesus mean when he instructs his followers to treat someone as a Gentile or a tax collector?

■ What is a one-sentence summary of Jesus' teaching in this Scripture?

### LET US PRAY

■ For all those who work to bring unity and reconciliation within the Church

■ For peacemakers

■ For honesty of heart

■ For all those who feel excluded from their families

■ For our own personal intentions (shared with the group or held silently before the Lord)

## A REFLECTIVE MOMENT OF SILENCE

## ADDITIONAL ACTIVITIES/DISCUSSION

■ How do we blend the common good and the good of the individual in our own faith community? in the world?

■ Let's make a list of specific peacemaking skills we can develop within our own faith community.

# Twenty-Fourth Sunday in
# ORDINARY TIME

*"...how often must I...?"*
Matthew 18:21

## WE GATHER IN PRAYER

Lord, teach us the real meaning of forgiveness. Show us how to extend forgiveness to others and to ask forgiveness for ourselves.

As we try one another's patience, O God, help us keep love as our primary motive...

# Amen

## READ MATTHEW 18:21-35

### REFLECT

Jesus teaches that there is no limit to the forgiveness Christians should have for one another. He tells a story to illustrate how forgiving we should be. We expect forgiveness ourselves—but are often short on forgiveness for others.

Forgiveness does not mean that we compromise our Christian principles. Forgiveness means we begin with love.

### CONSIDER

■ What is Jesus saying about the role of limits in the Christian lifestyle?

■ What is the significance of this Scripture to our faith journeys?

### LET US PRAY

■ For those who have been hurt unjustly

■ For those who are consumed by revenge

■ For the gifts of mercy, patience, and tolerance

■ For a greater appreciation of the sacrament of reconciliation

■ For our own personal intentions (shared with the group or held silently before the Lord)

## A REFLECTIVE MOMENT OF SILENCE

## ADDITIONAL ACTIVITIES/DISCUSSION

■ How does forgiving and being forgiven change us?

■ How could a greater sense of forgiveness make a difference in the world?

# Twenty-Fifth Sunday in
# ORDINARY TIME

*"Are you envious...?"*
Matthew 20:15

## WE GATHER IN PRAYER

Lord, thank you for your generous goodness, for sending us your Son, for the power of your word. Fill us with a generous spirit.

Untangle the hold of envy that limits our vision, O God, that we may extend and receive with a generous heart...

Amen

## READ MATTHEW 20:1-16

### REFLECT

This story of Jesus causes us to pause with a start. How can this be? How can those who have labored all day receive the same compensation as those who have labored only one hour? Is this fair?

Everything in our reason screams, "No, that's not fair!" Yet, our faith in God and the way we live out that faith are not based on "fair." There is nothing "fair" about the way God has ordered the world.

### CONSIDER
- Summarize the teaching in this parable.
- How was the landowner actually very fair?

### LET US PRAY
- For generosity
- For a genuine concern for the poor
- For the conversion of sinners
- For those who are trapped in their own greed
- For our own personal intentions (shared with the group or held silently before the Lord)

### A REFLECTIVE MOMENT OF SILENCE

### ADDITIONAL ACTIVITIES/DISCUSSION
- How does this Scripture make us feel?
- When have we been angry because someone was generous?

# Twenty-Sixth Sunday in
# ORDINARY TIME

*"What is your opinion?"*
Matthew 21:28

## WE GATHER IN PRAYER

Lord, thank you for the challenge of your word. Thank you for the invitation to search your word for meaning and relevance to our lives of faith.

Loosen the binds of narrow thinking that entrap us, O God. Fill us with honesty and truth...

### Amen

## READ MATTHEW 21:28-32

## REFLECT

Jesus tells a story to bring about change in the lives of the chief priests and elders. He asks their opinion about the two sons who respond to their father's command in different ways. One son says "Sure" but means "No"; the other says "No" but means "Sure."

Jesus says that tax collectors and harlots repented of their sins when John the Baptist preached to them. Their hearts were well-disposed. Jesus is trying to get the chief priests and elders to look at themselves.

## CONSIDER

■ Why does Jesus target this teaching to the chief priests and elders?

■ Why does Jesus start his teaching with "What is your opinion?" (21:28)

## LET US PRAY

■ For the grace of repentance

■ For the grace of perseverance

■ For the courage to confess our sins and change our lives

■ For the grace to pore over the word of God

■ For our own personal intentions (shared with the group or held silently before the Lord)

## A REFLECTIVE MOMENT OF SILENCE

## ADDITIONAL ACTIVITIES/DISCUSSION

■ How does procrastination deter us along our faith journeys?

■ How are we like chief priests and elders?

# Twenty-Seventh Sunday in
# ORDINARY TIME

*"...a people that will produce its fruit."*
Matthew 21:43

## WE GATHER IN PRAYER

Lord, clear away our prejudice and bias. Help us to hear your word with fresh awareness.

Thank you for calling us to yourself, O God, for opening the kingdom to those of us who constantly miss your call...

Amen

## READ MATTHEW 21:33-43

### REFLECT

This parable is about the religious establishment of Jesus' day. The householder, the workers, and the vineyard have to do with the kingdom of God. There is a comparison here. Throughout history, God has sent prophets and holy people. They have been treated badly and rejected.

Our challenge is to find our own role in this Scripture and to gain from it an overview of God's plan of salvation still unfolding today.

### CONSIDER

■ How are we the servants in this parable? the tenants? the son?

■ Summarize Jesus' teaching in this parable.

### LET US PRAY

■ For the gift of understanding

■ For an appreciation of God's extravagant love

■ For a greater knowledge of the Bible

■ For the wisdom to understand our own role in God's plan for salvation

■ For our own personal intentions (shared with the group or held silently before the Lord)

### A REFLECTIVE MOMENT OF SILENCE

### ADDITIONAL ACTIVITIES/DISCUSSION

■ How does our faith life show an appreciation for the kingdom of God?

■ When have we failed to appreciate the kingdom of God?

# Twenty-Eighth Sunday in
# ORDINARY TIME

*"...to summon the invited guests..."*
Matthew 22:3

## WE GATHER IN PRAYER

Lord, we hear your invitation. Jesus invites us; your holy word invites us. We long to respond.

Flood our souls with your grace. Help us see how blessed we are in knowing you. Let our faith be our delight...

### Amen

## READ MATTHEW 22:1-14

### REFLECT

Jesus teaches that everyone is invited to have a loving relationship with God. There is nothing compelling; there is no pressure. The invitation is freely given.

A generally accepted explanation of this story of the wedding banquet is that the "Chosen People," the Jews, did not receive Jesus as the Messiah. Thus, the invitation to enter the kingdom went to the Gentiles.

### CONSIDER

- Summarize Jesus' teaching in this parable?
- Why does Jesus use the vineyard as a frequent symbol in his parables?

### LET US PRAY

- For a firm belief in God's total acceptance
- For kindness and compassion for friends and acquaintances who are difficult
- For a spirit of hospitality
- For open hearts to accept God's grace
- For our own personal intentions (shared with the group or held silently before the Lord)

## A REFLECTIVE MOMENT OF SILENCE

## ADDITIONAL ACTIVITIES/DISCUSSION

- Does this parable fill us with dread? hope? confusion?
- How do we know if we're responding to God's invitation to enter the kingdom?

# Twenty-Ninth Sunday in
# ORDINARY TIME

*"Is it lawful...?"*
Matthew 22:17

## WE GATHER IN PRAYER

Lord, teach us how to live in a world that looks away from your teachings. Show us how to take your word into our daily lives.

Help us see Jesus as the way, the truth, and the life. Bless us with the gift of discernment...

# Amen

## READ MATTHEW 22:15-21

### REFLECT

Jesus was one of us. He knew the pressures of his followers' expectations; he knew the longings of those who loved him; he knew the pinch of bureaucratic red tape.

Jesus is not caught, however, in the trap set for him. He crosses no line that leaves him disloyal to the state. Yet, his response states clearly that human power has its limits.

### CONSIDER

■ How does Jesus "cover all his bases" when he responds to the Herodians?

■ What does Jesus tell us in his response to the Herodians?

## LET US PRAY

■ For patience and understanding

■ For the ability to discern the limits of human powers

■ For the grace to witness to Jesus in our daily lives

■ For the courage to demand the truth

■ For our own personal intentions (shared with the group or held silently before the Lord)

## A REFLECTIVE MOMENT OF SILENCE

## ADDITIONAL ACTIVITIES/DISCUSSION

■ How can we apply this teaching when paying our own taxes?

■ Do we ever use this teaching for our own gain?

# Thirtieth Sunday in
# ORDINARY TIME

*"You shall love..."*
Matthew 22:37

## WE GATHER IN PRAYER

Lord, bless us with a genuine realization of your commandment to love. Let it not pass overhead as a trite cliché.

Help us appreciate the path of love that takes us directly to you...

## Amen

## READ MATTHEW 22:34-40

### REFLECT

Jesus speaks in such simple terms. When he is asked which commandment is the greatest, he goes right to the heart of faith: love. Naturally, the Pharisees and Sadducees are disappointed. They aren't really interested in the commandments; they simply want to try one more angle of attack against Jesus.

The stifling limits of the Mosaic Law are given a breath of fresh air as Jesus focuses on love.

### CONSIDER

- Why does Jesus add a comment about the "second" great commandment?
- What is the significance of this teaching to our faith journeys today?

## LET US PRAY

- For loving hearts
- For all those who are afraid of love
- For self-discipline in the name of love
- For a respect of what the Ten Commandments mean
- For our own personal intentions (shared with the group or held silently before the Lord)

## A REFLECTIVE MOMENT OF SILENCE

## ADDITIONAL ACTIVITIES/DISCUSSION

- Are the Ten Commandments relevant today? If so, how? If not, why?
- How do we love God with all our heart? all our soul? all our mind?

# Thirty-First Sunday in
# ORDINARY TIME

*"You have but one teacher..."*
Matthew 23:8

## WE GATHER IN PRAYER

Lord, hold our eyes on you as our master, our teacher, our guide, our salvation. Grace us with the humility to be truthful always.

Lead us not into temptation. Dispose our wills that we may want only to please you...

### Amen

## READ MATTHEW 23:1-12

## REFLECT

Jesus tells the crowds that the scribes and Pharisees do not practice what they preach. There is a discrepancy between their words and their actions.

The people are burdened with a multitude of Mosaic laws. They hardly know which way to turn for fear of sin. Yet, those imposing the laws are able to find loopholes for themselves. Jesus explains that a truly great person is one who serves.

## CONSIDER

- Why does Jesus admonish his disciples to call no one "father"?
- What is Jesus teaching about power in this gospel?

## LET US PRAY

- For all those who volunteer to serve their communities with loyalty and love
- For all educators
- For all students
- For genuine humility that leads to genuine service
- For our own personal intentions (shared with the group or held silently before the Lord)

## A REFLECTIVE MOMENT OF SILENCE

## ADDITIONAL ACTIVITIES/DISCUSSION

- What does service mean in a Christian context?
- In practical terms, how are we truly servants to others?

# Thirty-Second Sunday in
# ORDINARY TIME

*"...went out to meet the bridegroom..."*
Matthew 25:1

## WE GATHER IN PRAYER

Lord, if we will but watch for your nearness to manifest itself, we will not miss you. Bless us with patience and insight to be watchful, wise, and prepared to receive you.

When we glimpse you, O God, fill us with rejoicing...

Amen

## READ MATTHEW 25:1-13

### REFLECT

Jesus teaches that there is a time when we will have to account for ourselves. He tells the story of the groom going to the bride's home to bring her to his own home. The bridesmaids, like bridesmaids today, wait.

Yet, some of the bridesmaids in Jesus' story wait unprepared. They're patient enough in their waiting, but they do not think ahead. They wait—but are not ready.

### CONSIDER

■ What is the significance of the groom's delay?

■ What does the oil symbolize?

### LET US PRAY

■ For the courage to look at our own foolishness

■ For an appreciation of the sacrament of reconciliation

■ For the insight to understand God's word as it affects our daily lives

■ For the grace to appreciate the spiritual opportunity to wait

■ For our own personal intentions (shared with the group or held silently before the Lord)

## A REFLECTIVE MOMENT OF SILENCE

## ADDITIONAL ACTIVITIES/DISCUSSION

■ How does our gathering each week teach us to wait like the virgins who had enough oil?

■ Do the virgins who had enough oil appear selfish?

# Thirty-Third Sunday in
# ORDINARY TIME

*"...to each according to his ability."*
Matthew 25:15

## WE GATHER IN PRAYER

Lord, thank you for the special gifts you've given each of us individually. May we respect those gifts by using them to your greater glory.

Bless our efforts with a balance in all things...

## Amen

## READ MATTHEW 25:14-30

## REFLECT

Jesus teaches that everyone is to make good use of their own individual talents. We all have good qualities and are endowed with certain abilities that are to be used and developed for God's honor and glory.

Notice how Jesus is specific about identifying the amount that each servant is given. This is an important element in understanding the wisdom of this parable. We cannot appreciate our gifts until we know what they are.

## CONSIDER

- There are three servants in this parable. How are we a little of each?
- Besides "lazy," how else might we describe the third servant?

## LET US PRAY

- For the grace to use our gifts to their fullest potential
- For the grace to know when we're overextending ourselves
- For the grace to call forth the gifts in others
- For the grace to admit our shortcomings
- For our own personal intentions (shared with the group or held silently before the Lord)

## A REFLECTIVE MOMENT OF SILENCE

## ADDITIONAL ACTIVITIES/DISCUSSION

- How can we help one another discern our own unique gifts?
- How can we tell if we're using our gifts to their fullest potential? beyond their potential?

# CHRIST THE KING

*"When the Son of Man comes..."*
Matthew 25:31

### WE GATHER IN PRAYER

Lord, we know you are mighty and just. Help us to trust in you as a loving God. Help us to fear you as a just God.

Show us how to be mindful of your grace, how to cooperate with you in kindness and compassion...

## Amen

### READ MATTHEW 25:31-46

### REFLECT

Jesus describes Judgment Day. Angels will assist Jesus, the Judge and King. Jesus uses the image of sheep and goats to explain the process of judging.

The process of separation is especially important in Jesus' explanation. It is not so much a separation of the "good" from the "bad," for sheep are not better than goats. Rather, it is a separation of those who recognize him, the Messiah, the Son of God, from those who do not.

### CONSIDER

■ Why is this Scripture significant for the feast of Christ the King?

■ What image of God does this Scripture create for us?

### LET US PRAY

■ For an appreciation of God's Good News as manifested in Jesus Christ

■ For all those who experience rejection in their attempts to spread the Good News

■ For those who are thirsty and hungry for the Good News

■ For a spirit of Christ in reaching out to others

■ For our own personal intentions (shared with the group or held silently before the Lord)

### A REFLECTIVE MOMENT OF SILENCE

### ADDITIONAL ACTIVITIES/DISCUSSION

■ How does this Scripture influence our lives on a day-to-day basis?

■ Are we good for the sake of goodness or for our own personal reward? Does it matter?

FEAST DAYS

# Our Lady's
# ASSUMPTION

*"...my spirit rejoices in God..."*
Luke 1:47

## WE GATHER IN PRAYER

Lord, may we turn to you with praise in the tremendous moments of our lives as well as in the ordinary and routine. Lift our hearts with hope and anticipation even when life seems disappointing.

Bless us with the gift of spontaneous prayer, just as Mary burst with praise for your goodness. Someday we hope to sing your praises for all eternity...

### Amen

## READ LUKE 1:39-56

## REFLECT

Mary is pregnant, yet she undertakes the long journey to visit her cousin, Elizabeth. When Mary and Elizabeth meet, joy quivers through the tiny infant in Elizabeth's womb; the first hosanna is sounded.

Mary's response is a spontaneous and innocent praise for God's boundless goodness and mercy. She doesn't clearly understand her role in salvation history, yet her faith energizes her and fills her with profound and prophetic praise. She knows the hunger for justice; she trusts in the mercy of God.

## CONSIDER

- Why has the Church chosen this passage for today's feast?
- Why is the Assumption of Our Lady significant in the history of salvation?

## LET US PRAY

- For a deeper devotion to Mary, the Mother of Jesus, the Mother of the Church
- For God's blessings on unborn infants, that their rights are protected by those who can speak for them
- For families, that their joy in one another will proclaim the goodness of the Lord
- For married couples, that grace will guide them in a life of passion and service
- For our own personal intentions (shared with the group or held silently before the Lord)

## A REFLECTIVE MOMENT OF SILENCE

## ADDITIONAL ACTIVITIES/DISCUSSION

- What are some accusations we've heard regarding our reverence for Mary? What might our responses be in the future?
- How do we emphasize the significance of Mary in our personal faith journeys?

# ALL SAINTS

## WE GATHER IN PRAYER

Lord, how can we imagine the extent of peace and contentment you offer us? You created us from love, for love, for yourself.

Quiet our hearts to hear the wisdom of your words: from mountaintops to desolate street corners, may we hear your voice and understand your words...

Amen

## READ MATTHEW 5:1-12

## REFLECT

Jesus notices that he has a listening crowd. He takes the opportunity to summarize the Good News. To the surprise of his listeners, however, Jesus speaks of the privileged state of those considered the least privileged: the poor, those who mourn, those who are hungry and thirsty, those who are persecuted.

Jesus' listeners hear just the opposite of what they expected. In their state of poverty, hunger, and oppression, they are blessed. They are blessed as they mourn. They are blessed in their persecutions.

## CONSIDER

- How might Jesus state the beatitudes for today's listeners?
- What is the significance of this event to the feast of All Saints?

## LET US PRAY

- For the wisdom to understand the rich truth of the beatitudes
- For the courage to embrace the beatitudes as directives for life
- For the humility to be truly poor in spirit
- For merciful hearts, that we may offer the love of God to others
- For our own personal intentions (shared with the group or held silently before the Lord)

## A REFLECTIVE MOMENT OF SILENCE

## ADDITIONAL ACTIVITIES/DISCUSSION

- How have we adopted the beatitudes in our daily lives?
- Let's discuss the "payoff" mentality that often plagues the Christian life: are we virtuous for our own gain or purely for the love of God?

# IMMACULATE CONCEPTION

*... the virgin's name was Mary.*
Luke 1:27

## WE GATHER IN PRAYER

Lord, thank you for the model of faithful goodness you have given us in Mary. In her simple, quiet way, she responded "Yes" to your invitation to risk, to face the unknown, to love.

Fashion our hearts with the faith of Mary. Teach us to trust your ways...

Amen

## READ LUKE 1:26-38

### REFLECT

Mary went about her quiet life with faith and hope. No doubt she had heard about the Promised One who would save her people from oppression—but little did she realize the role she would play.

Then the angel appears to her and invites her into an event that will change the world: "Behold, you will conceive in your womb and bear a son..." (1:31). To Mary, this is a confusing possibility because she isn't anyone's wife at the time. Yet, faced with public ridicule, Mary responds, "May it be done to me according to your word" (1:38).

### CONSIDER

- Do we understand that the feast of the Immaculate Conception does not celebrate Jesus' conception in Mary's womb but Mary's conception in the womb of her mother?
- Why does the Church celebrate the conception of Mary?

### LET US PRAY

- For a true appreciation of our baptismal vows
- For a devotion to Mary that reflects our trust in her role in salvation history
- For a willingness to respond "Yes" to all God's invitations
- For an appreciation of the Joyful, the Sorrowful, and the Glorious Mysteries
- For our own personal intentions (shared with the group or held silently before the Lord)

### A REFLECTIVE MOMENT OF SILENCE

### ADDITIONAL ACTIVITIES/DISCUSSION

- How has devotion to Mary changed over the years?
- Would we like to close this session with a decade of the rosary?

## Also Available...

**Exploring the Sunday Gospel Cycle B and Exploring the Sunday Gospel Cycle C.** *$6.95 each*

# Other Helpful Resources From Liguori Publications...

## A Catholic Guide to the Bible

*by Oscar Lukefahr, C.M.*

This book is written to help readers feel more confident when they consider studying the Bible. Author Father Oscar Lukefahr takes each of the 73 biblical books and offers a pertinent historical background, information about the biblical author and the literary style of the work, and a theological interpretation of selected passages. *$5.95*

(Workbook available—*$2.95*)

## "We Believe..."
### *A Survey of the Catholic Faith*

*by Oscar Lukefahr, C.M.*

This book offers a concise, contemporary explanation of Catholic teaching—including its roots in Scripture and living tradition. Author Father Lukefahr also includes creative analogies to help readers understand the relevance of traditional Catholic beliefs in today's world. *$5.95*

(Workbook available—*$2.95*)

## Praying in the Catholic Tradition

*by Peter Schineller, SJ*

In this booklet, Father Schineller helps readers explore their prayer possibilities. He offers basic information about prayer, guidelines for prayer, and ways to pray in the Catholic tradition. With this booklet, both new and cradle Catholics can build an active and fulfilling personal prayer life. *$3.95*

## Yielding
### *Prayers for Those in Need of Hope*

*by William J. O'Malley, SJ*

Scripture passages and great works of literature are fused together with original prayers to fashion a unique 30-day plan of daily (morning, midday, and evening) prayers. Those who are wrestling with difficulty will find renewed hope in this book. *$6.95*

Order from your local bookstore or write to
**Liguori Publications**
Box 060, Liguori, MO 63057-9999
*(Please add $1 for postage and handling for orders under $5; $1.50 for orders over $5.)*
For faster service call toll-free (800) 325-9521, ext. 060.
Please have Visa or MasterCard ready.